Billie Kaye Tsika

OPERATION
BLESSING

SPEAKING BLESSINGS
INTO THE LIVES OF OUR FAMILIES

Billie Kaye Tsika

OPERATION BLESSING

SPEAKING BLESSINGS
INTO THE LIVES OF OUR FAMILIES

Plow On Publications
www.plowon.org

Plow On Publications
a division of Paul E. Tsika Ministries, Inc.
Restoration Ranch
P. O. Box 136
Midfield, TX   77458

www.plowon.org

Printed in the United States of America

dedication

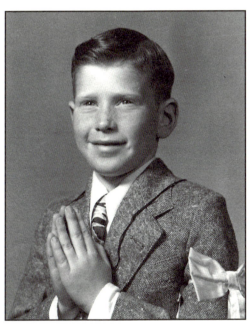

Paul at his first communion. Is he a sweetheart or what!

I am dedicating this book to you, my husband. You have been my main source of blessing on this earth. You have encouraged me so many times in our years together. When I began to think about getting serious with my singing, you were the one who encouraged me to practice, practice, and practice. Even though you were my biggest critic, you were also my biggest encourager and fan. When I began to do some speaking, you were there to encourage me and help me get my mind together. As I began this book, you were there to inspire me and 'nudge' me to get it finished.

You are a great giver, not just in temporal things, but in those things that are eternal.

I appreciate the heart that you have to repent and 'plow on' through every situation. I am thankful for a man who doesn't 'moan' and 'groan' or wallow in self pity, but gets up and starts making right choices. You have taught me much about believing that our God is a God of mercy and grace and forgiveness.

I know this one thing; God put us together in 1966 with an express purpose. We will never know the full extent of His purpose, but thank you for having a heart to want to please and serve Christ and a determination to fulfill His purpose for us on this earth.

We've walked together through many good times and some bad times, the sad times and the mad times, the joyful times and the grieving times, the hurtful times and the healing times. I know God has used every situation to bring us closer to Him. Nothing has been wasted! All things work together for our good and God's glory, because we love Him, and what the enemy means for evil, God means for good. Hallelujah!

Without you in my life, I would not be who I am today. I love your sense of humor. You make me laugh. I love your ability to bring hope and happiness when I'm discouraged or upset. God has used you to provide for me, and I might say greatly provide for me. You have loved me with a great love; you have encouraged me with words of wisdom. Because of the ministry God has given you, I have had doors open for my ministry in speaking, singing and opportunities to minister to hurting women. You have given me three wonderful children. When I think about it, I really don't know where I would be without you. You, more than anyone else, are the instrument that God is using to make me more like Jesus. You are my 'heavenly' sandpaper. For this, I am eternally grateful. Thank you for being a blessing these 42 years.

acknowledgements

A special thanks to:

Wade Trimmer, my wonderful friend and pastor, for his contribution to this book of blessings.

Cynthia L. Watke, for cover and book design.

Gary Wright, Mercury Press, for his faithful friendship and support of our ministry in all of our printing needs.

Andrea Blaho, for proofing this manuscript.

preface

Never, never, never, in your life could you have convinced me, when I was a teenager that I would be living this life of blessing that I am living today!

Actually, I wasn't even thinking about God's blessings during my growing up years, because I was too preoccupied, totally consumed and absorbed with ME. I wanted to get away and do my own thing. Eleven days after I graduated from high school in 1965, I left for the Marine Corps.

Paul and I met in the Marine Corps in 1966, and little did I know what God had in store for us. After dating for a month and a half, we got married. We were discharged in the fall of 1966 and headed to Maine where Paul was born and raised. His parents lived in Sanford, so we settled there.

The four years we lived in Maine were very rough years. Even though Paul worked and took care of me (and two children by this time) financially, he spent much of his time drunk and living wicked. He, of course, was not a Christian at this time.

God engineered the circumstance that necessitated us moving to Texas. It was there that Paul eventually heard the gospel of Jesus Christ and was gloriously 'born again.' Our life began to change, even though we would walk through rough waters for a few more years. Although I was a religious person, I didn't come to meet the Lord in a personal and saving way until 1974 -- three years after Paul gave his heart to the Lord.

Paul knew God had called him to preach, so he began to travel with an evangelist and minister wherever God opened doors. I, of course, stayed home to raise the children. We lived from week to week when it came to finances, but we never went without! We always had a roof over our heads and food to eat. Admittedly, our cupboards were not stocked full, but we never went hungry as God always provided.

We moved to Louisiana in 1975 with very little material things to take with us. When we drove through Oklahoma, we stopped to visit a dear friend who was gracious and gave us a car. We moved into a brick home, without furniture, because we had given ours away before leaving Texas. However, God provided a tremendous 'love offering' from a church in Uvalde, Texas when Paul preached a meeting there. We were able to purchase the furniture we needed and use the excess to 'live' for the next few months.

God began to open doors for Paul to preach meetings. Even though most people would have considered us 'poor,' we felt we were blessed by the Lord. He provided for us and sustained us. He opened doors of ministry for Paul and provided the finances. He gave us new friends, and He gave our family a wonderful church to be a part of, which was a blessing when Paul was away.

As the years flew by our daughter, Gretchen, met her soul mate at Liberty University in Virginia. She and Mark were married in 1987. This was a tremendous blessing. We praise God for such a wonderful, godly son-in-law who loves our daughter and provides for her and their three girls.

In 1988, Paul, Paul Edward, Thom and I moved to North Carolina. Paul Edward and Melanie were making wedding plans at this time, yet Paul Edward moved with us without saying a negative word or refusing to go. This was a blessing. They were married June 2, 1988 in Louisiana. We don't consider Melanie a daughter-in-law, but a daughter. She is a great blessing to our whole family and a wonderful mother to four of our grandchildren.

Thom was 16 years old when we moved him from his lifelong friends, so we began to pray that God would let him meet a friend. It wasn't long before he and Kelley met at Grassy Branch Baptist Church in Asheville, where we then made our home. They dated until their wedding in March of 1991. God is so good. He blessed us with another fantastic daughter whom we love and treasure. She is a faithful wife, a gifted painter and decorator, and a great mom to Shelby, Jake and Kadie Jewel.

At this juncture in our lives, Paul and I were now what some call "empty-nesters." Our children were all married and having children! How blessed can two people be? We headed out on the road to do revival meetings together. God provided a wonderful van for us to travel in, so we packed everything we needed into that van. We traveled from East to West and

North to South. God was so faithful to provide so many churches in which to minister. When we would get back to our condo in Asheville, we didn't even unpack. We just lived out of our suitcases.

At this time, we decided we needed to live on the road, so in 1993 we sold our condo in Asheville and purchased a beautiful Prevost Bus. This was definitely a provision from the Lord. Of course, He used many generous people to help us. We lived and traveled in our bus until 2005. These were some of the greatest years of our lives. We felt so blessed by the Lord to have a home on the road all those years.

In October 1995, Paul and I were at a Bible conference at Grace Fellowship in Augusta, Georgia. At this particular meeting, God chose to heal me from chronic back pain that I had struggled with for many years. I can not tell you how thankful I am to the God of Creation for reaching down that night and healing me. How blessed I am that He would consider me. We fell in love with the pastor of Grace, whom we had known for a few years. Wade Trimmer and his wife Anne welcomed us into their fellowship with open arms. We joined the following year. We are still members of Grace Fellowship and great friends with Wade and Anne.

When we began to travel to California in the early 90s, we met a wonderful couple, Jim and Judy Head, who introduced us to a whole new realm of ministry. We began to minister to their business organization by doing marriage counseling and marriage seminars. Paul began to do some motivational speaking using principles from God's Word and to preach on Sunday mornings to their organization. This began to change our hearts about ministry! We had more of a desire to minister one-on-one to the precious people in this group than in churches. It's amazing how God begins to change a person's heart when He gets ready to change their direction.

We had a choice to make. Knowing we couldn't continue to travel and preach revival meetings as we had been doing for so many years and also do ministry with this organization, we found our hearts being turned toward this very different ministry. We call it Marketplace Ministry. Many of our pastor friends felt like we had 'left' the ministry. However, we stay busier in every aspect of this ministry than we ever did in the previous years.

In January 2000, Paul and I purchased 80 acres in Midfield, Texas (about 20 minutes from the Gulf of Mexico). Little did we know what God had planned for us when we bought this parcel of land in South Texas. We wanted to have a place for the children and grandchildren to come to when we were 'home.'

Shortly after we purchased our property, Ron and Georgia Lee Puryear, along with the Management Team of World Wide Dream Builders of Spokane, Washington, asked Paul to come on board as their pastor/advisor. This was quite a surprise, but we knew immediately that this was God's doing. As Paul and I talked about this offer, we knew that God had prepared us for this position. Knowing that God had used every situation in our lives, good and bad, to prepare us for this type of ministry, we joyfully accepted this position with these wonderful people.

Meanwhile, back on the Ranch, we began to build...and build....and build. We built a pavilion, a shed, a barn, cabins (one for Mark and Gretchen, one for Paul and Melanie and one for Thom and Kelley), corrals for our horses and an office. Paul Edward and Melanie built a home. Thom and Kelley built a home, and then we built the Lodge where Paul and I live.

As we began to minister in this organization, we felt it would benefit couples to come to the Ranch when counseling was needed, so we offered the cabins to those who wanted and needed help in their marriages and relationships. This keeps us quite busy when we're not traveling to functions held by World Wide. We love what we do and the people with whom we have been blessed to spend what we trust will be the rest of our lives.

Now in our sixties, Paul and I feel more blessed than ever. Aware that this is the last season of our life, we are intent upon seeing it bring more glory to God and good to people than we could have ever hoped for. We pray that it will transfer to the next generation as well. Paul has said, "You don't have to invent a dream. You will discover it as you walk in faith and obedience." Dreams do come true! We are blessed and very much so.

Paul and Billie Kaye on their wedding day, April 28, 1966.
Port Royal Baptist Church, Beaufort, SC. I wasn't unhappy, but I was scared!

why a book of blessings?

Originally, the purpose of writing this book was for my children and grandchildren so that they would come to know how blessed they are, and why they are so blessed. Knowing that the weakest ink is better than the strongest memory, I also wanted to bless them verbally and in written form, so that they could be continually reminded of their worth, even after I am gone. I wanted them to know they can reach for the stars…and really 'reach' them. I wanted them to know that God has made them to prosper in every area of their lives and to understand that He has put in every one of His children the ability to live life to the fullest. I wanted them to 'hear' with their hearts that God has a plan for their lives, and that He wants to bless them exceedingly, abundantly above anything they can ask or even think. I wanted them to know what God's Word says, and then live their lives accordingly.

Social Science did a study about the number of times a child heard the word 'no.' By the time a child is five years old, they have heard the word 'no' approximately 40,000 times and the word 'yes' only 8,000 times! This is far too lopsided for me! Now, I know we have to train children and saying no is a vital part of their growing years. No is a necessary word — "No, don't go there! No, don't eat that! No, don't hit your sister! Don't! Don't! Don't! No! No! No!" With my children, I never really thought about this constant flow of no's. However, with my grandchildren, I am no longer ignorant of the importance of this information! So, I want to balance this with letting them know what they can do and what they can accomplish by blessing them. There are many things that are, yes. Yes! Yes! Yes! Their little brains have been so bombarded with hearing "no" so many times that they take this negativism into adulthood thinking they can't do anything with their life. They replay those negativisms. "You're too dumb; you're too awkward; you're too poor; you're too skinny; you'll never amount to anything; you're a troublemaker; you're so mean; etc." Then they act on the lies of the enemy rather than the truth of God.

We all like to hear how well we're doing or how great we are. I have heard so many women say about their child, "He's/she's so mean." "He/she is so clumsy." "He is so lazy." When children hear what Mom or Dad say about them, they endeavor to live up to what is said. When children hear what teachers, preachers, aunts, uncles and the adults they admire say about them, they are greatly influenced. It's amazing how much a child wants to please their parents and be affirmed by them. If you say, "He's a great reader," then that child will likely read continually to prove you right. If you say, "He's a great runner," then that child will more than likely take off running around the house. Why don't we try this on our family, children, friends and grandchildren? Acknowledge some act of kindness. Tell them how you depend on them and how much it means to you for them to keep the trash emptied, or let them know how they bless you when they clean the kitchen. I believe you will be amazed at their desire to be appreciated, acknowledged, affirmed and thanked. Why is it that we feel like we have to 'pick out' the negative instead of encouraging the positive? Maybe, it's because we heard the negative so many times as a child and have never learned how to be positive in our affirmation. Well, it's time to change!! It's time to learn how to bless our children, grandchildren, friends and family. It's time for the 'blessings' to flow, because we have all heard too many 'negatives' in our lifetime.

Having said all this, my prayer is that this little book of blessings will help you begin to bless everyone you know, especially your children. Start somewhere and start now! Women, this works great on your husbands. They love to know (verbally) how much you appreciate them; how much you depend on them to provide and care for you; how 'strong' they are! Guys, women need to hear they are loved. You can't tell them the day you're married and expect it to last 40 years. They need to hear it daily. They need to know you cherish them and appreciate them for keeping your house clean, for raising your children, for doing your laundry and all the 'stuff' that comes with parenting...day after day after day. Teach your children how to bless each other on a daily basis, and start by being a 'pattern' for them to follow.

May you be blessed as you begin to act like Father God and be a blessing and a "blesser" of others!

table of contents

chapter 1
What is our basis for blessing?

"**G**od bless you" is a common three-word phrase used in every section of American culture today. Some people say a "blessing" before they eat a meal while others say, "Bless you," after someone sneezes. Whether religious or not, people around the world will claim to either be a blessing or have been blessed by something or someone in their life.

In many churches, as the time of corporate worship comes to a conclusion, the pastor raises his hands and speaks a blessing over the congregation: *"The Lord bless you and keep you, the Lord make His face shine upon you and be gracious to you, the LORD turn His face toward you and give you peace."* Numbers 6:24-26

> *When you have an attitude of gratitude, blessings automatically flow.*
> Billie Kaye Tsika

Various cultures have different types of blessings. For example, there is an Irish blessing for children that says, "May God be with you and bless you. May you see your children's children. May you be poor in misfortunes and rich in blessings. May you know nothing but happiness from this day forward."

Another Irish blessing says, "May you be in heaven thirty minutes before the devil knows you are dead!"

What do we mean by the use of such expressions as, "God bless you," or "I bless you in Jesus' name," or "Be blessed?" Is it just an expression that is uttered out of an unknown tradition or as a superstitious use for avoiding bad luck? Is it a harmless expression that is synonymous with "Have a good day?" Is it just a means of creating or conveying a sort of warm-fuzzies type feeling in the hearts of other persons?

Is there a Biblical basis for the practice of "blessing" that has a supernatural significance and the potential for producing supernatural results? Yes! "Blessing" is a Biblical concept and is the privilege and duty of all Christians today.

Cherish
to treasure, adore, value and love

Quite often we hear people testifying about the many and varied blessings they receive in life — and they are truly varied depending upon the view of the persons. A Catholic priest, a Rabbi and a Presbyterian were discussing when the blessing of life began. The Catholic priest said, "It begins at conception." The Rabbi said, "The blessing of life begins at birth." The Presbyterian said, "The blessing of life begins when your children leave home!"

However, in Scripture, a "blessing" is a covenant provision and promise of God's abundant protection, so that His people can live all their lives under the purposeful, protective, provisionary and watchful care of their great God. Reading the Old Testament leads one to the obvious conclusion that God's blessing endues one with power for success, prosperity, and longevity of life. God's intention and desire to bless humanity is a central focus of His covenant relationships. For this reason, the concept of blessing pervades the Biblical record. Two distinct ideas are present. First, a blessing was a public declaration of a favored status with God. Second, the blessing endowed power for prosperity and success. In all cases, the blessing served as a guide and motivation to pursue a course of life within the blessing.

Even the most casual reading of God's Word reveals that He, the Blessed God, is the Author of all blessings. Previous generations did what is seldom, if ever, done in Christian homes today, i.e. daily speaking blessings over the family and home in the name of Father, Son, and Holy Spirit. This privilege and duty is now reserved almost exclusively to the clergy. This should not be so! It is time for this priestly duty of blessing, based upon the priesthood of all believers (1 Peter 2:9), to be restored so that our families, friends, and our society may experience more fully the impartation of God's goodness and grace.

What is the meaning of blessing? Webster's Dictionary defines "to bless" as meaning, "To invoke divine favor on, to bestow happiness, prosperity or good things of all kinds; to make a pronouncement holy; to consecrate, to glorify for the benefits received, to extol for excellencies." Webster's then defines a "Blessing" as, "A prayer or solemn wish imploring happiness upon another; a benediction or blessing; the act of pronouncing a benediction or blessing; that which promotes prosperity and welfare..."

Our English word "blessing" is derived from the Old English word "bleodsian" or "bletsian," which originally meant "sprinkling with blood" during the pagan sacrifices.

However, since the Bible was not written in English, but Hebrew and Greek, we must go to the scriptures themselves and to proper lexicons to determine the meaning.

The most common Old Testament Hebrew word translated "bless" is the word "barak." In the New Testament, the word "bless" often translates "makarios," meaning "blessed, fortunate, happy." Another New Testament Greek word is "eulegetos" (euologize) which means "to speak well of."

To bless means to speak good rather than evil, to encourage rather than discourage, to project success rather than failure, to give faith rather than doubt, to instill boldness rather than fear, to impart hope rather than distress, and to share love rather than neglect.

In the Scriptures, when the Hebrew word "barak," "to bless," is used in association with God, it means, "to bow with bended knee in order to

HAPPY 1. having, showing or causing great joy and pleasure 2. *an emotion characterized by sense of well-being and gladness* 3. CAUSING ONE TO SMILE

express awe and worth." Dr. Lynn Reddick gives insight into the richness of the Hebrew word most frequently translated "bless" —"Barak:" "The word "barak" paints a graphic word picture of a camel kneeling to eat and rest. While in this position, the camel can be loaded with cargo—goods that will bless other people. Likewise, as you rest in God's promises (some 8,000 promises are in the Bible), you are loaded with blessings as you learn to hear Him speak specific blessings for you and other people."

A wonderful definition of the meaning of the blessing of God is given by John Calvin: "The blessing of God is the goodness of God in action, by which a supply of all good pours down to us from His favor, as from its only fountain."

BLESSING AND CURSING are important Biblical concepts as reflected in the 516 uses of words such as bless (used 132 times), blessed (285), blesses (10), blessing (70), and blessings (19); and the 199 occurrences of such words as curse (97), cursed (74), curses (19), and cursing (9).

In the scriptures, blessing takes the form of three main types; God blessing man, man blessing God, and man blessing man.

treasure (trezh´er) 1. accumulated wealth 2. something of great worth 3. irreplaceable; priceless *forever*

chapter 2
Where do we find our basis for blessing?

According to Old Testament concepts, the formally spoken word had both an independent existence and the power of its own fulfillment. The word once spoken assumed a history of its own, almost a personality of its own. The word also had the power of its own fulfillment. These concepts are demonstrated in the prophet Isaiah's emphasis on God's Word:

> *Reflect upon your present blessings, of which every man has plenty; not on your past misfortunes of which all men have some.*
> Charles Dickens, author

Isaiah 55:10-11, *"For as the rain and the snow come down from heaven and do not return there but water the earth, making it bring forth and sprout, giving seed to the sower and bread to the eater, so shall my word be that goes out from my mouth; it shall not return to me empty, but it shall accomplish that which I purpose, and shall succeed in the thing for which I sent it."* The implication is that the Word that God speaks exists as a reality and has within itself the power of

its own fulfillment. Formal words of blessing or cursing also had the same power of self-fulfillment. When Isaac mistakenly blessed Jacob rather than Esau, he could not recall the blessing, for it existed in history (read Genesis 27:18-41); it had acquired an identity of its own. Blessing and cursing released supernatural power which could bring to pass the content of the curse or the blessing.

The author, Bill Gothard states that, "Throughout Scripture, the importance of verbal blessings is expressed. In four New Testament books, God gives us direct instruction to bless those who curse and revile us. When we obey His instruction, it produces results that are not expected by the one who gave the curse or the one who was cursed."

A verbal blessing is made up of three powerful forces: our words, God's Word, and God's name. The power of our words alone is affirmed by the Scripture that states, *"Death and life are in the power of the tongue."* (Proverbs 18:21) If we use our tongue properly, it will be a tree of life. Proverb 15:4 says, *"A wholesome tongue is a tree of life; but perverseness is a breach of spirit."* The translation in the Message is, *"Kind words heal and help; cutting words wound and maim."* We can give wisdom, speak kindness, give true courage and bring healing with our tongues. However, when we use our tongues improperly, the result is death; death to friendships, death to a marriage, devastation to a dream and hurts and wounds to our families.

PRECIOUS (presh´·es) 1. of great worth 2. beloved; cherished

A wonderful picture (there are many) of this truth on the power of the tongue is found in the Old Testament. In Numbers chapters 13-14, we read where God used Moses to lead the Israelites out of Egypt and into the Promised Land. Moses sent twelve men to spy out the land. He wanted them to find out everything they could about this place that God had promised them and bring back a report. They spent forty days walking through the land. They came back with their report. Ten of the spies said the land did flow with milk and honey, and the fruit was so huge that two men had to carry one bunch of grapes between them on a staff. But then the ten spies said, *"Nevertheless, the people are strong that dwell in the land, and the cities are walled, and very great; and moreover we saw the children of Anak (the giants) there."* However, two of the spies, Joshua and Caleb, would not go along with this evil report. *"And Caleb stilled the people before Moses, and said, let us go up at once, and possess it; we are well able to overcome it."* But, once again the ten said that they weren't able to go up against the people. One set of spies said, "We can do it." The majority said, "We can not go up against these people." All the people believed the negative report. This angered God because of their lack of faith and trust in Him.

As you read in Numbers 14:28, God said, *"As truly as I live, says the LORD, as you have spoken in my ears, so will I do to you."* So, what the ten spies said, they got. *"Their carcasses shall fall in the wilderness,"* but not only the ten. All who believed the evil report would die in the wilderness, never to experience the Promised Land. These two men, Joshua and Caleb, who believed that God could and would give them the Promised Land no matter the circumstances they would face, received what they declared.... *"As you have spoken in my ears, so will I do to you."* The tongue is a mighty force.

Professor David Stubbs states that a blessing is, "...a calling for the Holy Spirit to come and transform us." He writes that being blessed by God means that we become holy, reflective of God and the purposes of God. We need to be aware of the fact that there is clearly something more to a blessing than just a kind word spoken for encouragement or as an expression of gratitude for kind deeds. Blessings given in the Bible affirm that the words we speak in either blessing or cursing are powerful and potentially transforming in our attitudes so as to make us holy and reflective of God.

Professor John Chasteen writes, "The Biblical concept of blessing is foreign to the Western mindset." We comprehend blessing as "an earned commodity." The Hebrews understood it as favor, a bestowed gift, and approval, not based on merit or works done.

God taught the Jews to bless or approve their children not based on their merit or worth, but based on the fact that they belonged to God. Abraham blessed Isaac. Isaac blessed Jacob. Jacob blessed his twelve, and so the blessing was passed down.

The concept of blessing as it relates to families was never meant to be a quick fix. It was a lifestyle - a daily, weekly, and monthly thing. It had a prophetic element to it and was ordained from heaven. It consisted of five elements:

1) A meaningful touch
2) Meaningful spoken words or message
3) Attaching high value to the one being blessed
4) The picturing of a special future for the one being blessed
5) An active commitment to fulfill the blessing.

Someone well observed, "Jewish families know the importance of the blessing. A ceremony called a Bar Mitzvah is held when the male child is 13 years of age; the father speaks blessings over the child validating him for who he is in God. It is no accident that reports show that among all the criminals incarcerated, less than one percent are of Jewish heritage. The blessing of God can carry more power than the curse; His blessing is for a thousand generations and the curse for only four!"

Pastor John Hagee writes, "It is God's will to bless you! Not because you deserve it. God does not love you because of what you do. Jesus Christ paid the price for your sins. God blesses you, because He has chosen to bless you. His grace knows no limit. His love knows no measure. His compassion has no boundary. His tender mercies are renewed every morning."

Pastor Hagee then asks, "What is the blessing?" to which he gives an excellent definition. "The blessing is the impartation of the supernatural power of God into a human life by the spoken Word of God's delegated authority. It is God's will to bless every aspect of your life."

This supernatural blessing is invoked by speaking it aloud. Once the blessing has been spoken, it cannot be withdrawn! Only God can stop it for disobedience; no man can stop it. Once a spiritual authority speaks the blessing, you should fully expect it on your life.

Remember that the source of any blessing should be the Lord, and that a supernatural power is released when we bless and praise His Holy name.

Psalms 66:1-2, *"Make a joyful shout to God, all the earth! Sing out the honor of His name; make His praise glorious."*

In his book *The Power of the Spoken Blessing*, Bill Gothard includes a letter that his office received from a couple in New Zealand about how verbal blessing transformed a sad seven-year-old boy:

"My husband and I noticed our seven-year-old son Samuel was becoming characterized by a very miserable countenance, drooping shoulders, lips that go down instead of up, etc. Every attempt we made to correct the problem failed. We had reached the point of exasperation!

It was around this time that we listened to two audiotapes by Bill Ligon, titled *How to Impart Blessings* and *Redemptive Power of the Blessing*. We also watched a video on the power of the spoken word and read the book, *The Power of Spoken Blessings*, by Bill Gothard. Also, we saw the exciting video, *How to Transform Attitudes With Spoken Blessings*, by Chris and Anne Hogan. Through these materials, the Lord opened our understanding of the power of the spoken word, either as a blessing or a curse.

I remember the exciting revelation the Lord gave: "Samuel needs a blessing!"

I gathered the other children around and blessed Samuel. I asked God to bless him with a radiant countenance, joy in his heart, and a beautiful smile that ministered to the lives of others.

As I was speaking, his little face lit up, his chest puffed out, and he just

love (luv) a strong, deep affection and devotion for another, unconditional and unexplained

kept smiling! I spoke that same blessing to him once more that same week.

It has been around six months now, and I am very happy to report that the change in Samuel has been miraculous! He keeps smiling, has a radiant joy about him, and the first thing we notice about Samuel in the morning is a beautiful, radiant smile and a very enthusiastic "Good morning!" This has truly been a work of the Lord, for all of our own efforts failed. In simple faith, we have been obedient and have witnessed the power of the spoken blessing!

We have noticed several things happen in our family as we apply the lessons learned in giving a blessing. We are all demonstrating more love toward each other. Our attitudes really are transformed by speaking blessings, and the children are growing in faith!

Our children will come to us and report that one of their siblings needs a blessing because he/she has a bad attitude, or we should bless this child because he/she is being naughty!

All of us then gather around and bless the "offender." This act demonstrates great love toward him/her. No need for telling tales or taking matters into their own hands, as they now have a practical solution to the situation!

Whenever my husband and I notice a wrong attitude in a child, that child receives a blessing, and I am continually amazed at how attitudes are changed immediately! Sometimes a little talk is required, but the spoken blessing is the transformer.

As a practical aid to help the younger children make blessing others a part of their daily lives, we have included "give a blessing to a family member" on their job chart. This is working wonderfully!

Our five-year-old blesses his two-year-old sister every day. It usually goes like this: "The Lord bless you, Danielle, with courage, 'wise-ness' (wisdom), and knowledge!"

Our seven-year-old is blessing his ten-year-old brother to be diligent in his piano practice and blesses him to get through (survive) washing the dishes!

We can testify to both the power of the spoken blessing and the power of the spoken curse. We have experienced freedom from many spoken curses on our lives through speaking specific blessings. This Biblical principle has been life-changing and an answer to our many cries for help."

Craig Hill, the director of *Family Foundations International* of Littleton, Colorado, makes this observation about the tragic results of parents in general and fathers in particular who do not faithfully speak God's blessings upon their children: "Today, there is a lack of fathering and a lack of blessing and impartation, so people go in search of that blessing and of that manhood in all sorts of other ways. Some people go and join gangs - searching to become a man or a woman. Gangs, of course, have rites and mechanisms and ways that you can be accepted as a man or as a woman, by which you become a full-fledged member of that "family," so to speak. That happens when blessing doesn't legitimately take place through a father. Other people go in search of love and impartation through sexual promiscuity. Some people are drawn into homosexuality - young men in search of the love and impartation that really should have come from a father. Others are drawn into sexual promiscuity with the opposite gender. Many types of things take place that are destructive maladies in our society today that pass from one generation to the next when blessings have not been imparted. And where there has been impartation and blessing and the release of identity and destiny to children, you see just the opposite result. These things will flow from one generation to the next. In other words, we tend to do to our children and treat our children in similar ways that we have been treated by our parents."

With wise Biblical counsel, Pastor John Hagee writes, "The future of America will not be determined by presidents or politicians, but instead by what parents teach or fail to teach their children. Therefore, bless your children in the name of the Lord. Release the power of God into their lives with spoken blessings.

Lay your hands on them and speak healing into their mind and body. Speak confidence, success, love, joy, and peace. Shape their lives through the power of the blessing!

Parents, you are the priesthood of the home. You cannot change what you will not confront. Take charge of your children's lives through the power of the blessing, or Satan will."

Consider the power of the parental blessing. As parents, you have the power to speak life or death into the lives of your children. Parent, when you call your son or daughter "stupid," "idiot," "dumbbell," you have placed a curse upon their ability and motivation to learn! Speak words of life over and into them....blessings not cursings.

BELIEVE (be·leve') 1. to put one's trust in   2. to accept as fact   3. to have faith in   *togetherness*

chapter 3
How do we join God in this undertaking?

Our children have been married 21, 20 and 17 years. Our daughter, Gretchen is married to Mark and they have three girls. They live in Highland, California. Mark serves as Executive Pastor at Immanuel Baptist Church in Highland. Our two sons, Paul Edward and Thom work with us at the ranch, along with their wives and seven of our 10 grand children. We have tried to practice what I'm writing, and as I see the results, it is so encouraging. Believe me, dear friend, we know it's God's grace. However, God expects us to cooperate.

> *Count your blessings instead of your crosses;*
> *Count your gains instead of your losses.*
> *Count your joys instead of your woes;*
> *Count your friends instead of your foes.*
> *Count your smiles instead of your tears;*
> *Count your courage instead of your fears.*
> *Count your full years instead of your lean;*
> *Count your kind deeds instead of your mean.*
> *Count your health instead of your wealth;*
> *Count on God instead of yourself.*
> Author unknown

It is not enough to study, theorize, or lecture about the importance of blessings without personally developing the discipline of verbalizing those blessings, especially over our loved ones.

The following are blessings that were composed for, spoken over, and prayed over our children and grandchildren. However, they are generic enough to be used by you in doing the same for your friends and loved ones, as well as your grandchildren. Also, even as you are reading them, I ask our wonderful, faithful, promise-keeping Father to make them a special blessing to you!"

When our first grandchild, Meagan Ashley Rush, burst forth into this world, it was one of the greatest joys of our lives. Here was this little bundle of joy ready to face life. However, she had some struggling to do. She spent so much time in ICU in Denver, Colorado and was poked and prodded by every nurse and doctor. Twice she was rushed to the emergency room with her little body already blue. But God!! At the writing of this book, she is a joy-filled 19 year old getting ready to graduate from high school. God has a plan for her. She isn't afraid to speak up for the Lord. She tells everyone she is a Christian and is going to live her life for the One who saved her....both physically and spiritually.

blessing of thirst

The Blessing: "I bless you _____ with a heart-hunger that causes you to cry to the Lord your God. May He bless you with such favor that you see His power and glory when you cry unto Him. I bless you with a heart that will seek Him each morning and know from daily experience His loving kindness. May you bless the Lord as long as you live. May you be blessed with a heart that is so ravished by His love that your soul is satisfied with abundance as you praise Him with joyful lips. As a small deer pants for water, may your soul thirst for the true and living God."

Psalm 63:1-5 *God—you're my God! I can't get enough of you! I've worked up such hunger and thirst for God, traveling across dry and weary deserts. So here I am in the place of worship, eyes open, drinking in your strength and glory. In your generous love I am really living at last! My lips brim praises like fountains. I bless you every time I take a breath; My arms wave like banners of praise to you.* (The Message)

John 6:35 *And Jesus said, I am the bread of life. He who comes to Me shall never hunger, and he who believes in Me shall never thirst.* (ESV)

Psalm 107:9 *He satisfies those who are thirsty and fills the hungry with good things.* (ESV)

Another little blessing, Catherine Emily Tsika, came along in 1991 while Paul and Melanie were in Bible school in North Carolina. I walked the floor with Melanie while she waited 'patiently' for this precious gift from God. She was a little fireball with big blue eyes and blond hair. She definitely has a mind of her own, yet she honors her father and mother. She has a zest for life and is involved in every athletic event in school. We know God has wonderful plans for her future as she walks in His ways and allows Him to direct her path.

blessing of deliverance

The Blessing: "I bless you _____with the daily awareness that God is your shield and defender. I bless you with the confidence that comes from loving and serving a merciful God who meets you when you call to Him. May you be blessed with lips that sing of His power and His mercy. May you always know that He is your defense and refuge in your day of troubles. I bless you with the desire to be as free as Jesus died to make you. May you know that the Truth that sets you free is not propositions or principles but an ever-deepening love relationship with a Person – Jesus – the Truth and the Life."

Revelation 12:11 *They conquered him by the blood of the Lamb and by the word of their testimony, for they did not love their lives even in the face of death.* (ESV)

John 8:32, 36 *And you will know the truth, and the truth will set you free. So if the Son sets you free, you will be free indeed!* (ESV)

Isaiah 61:1 *The Spirit of the Lord GOD is upon me, because the LORD has anointed me to bring good news to the poor; He has sent me to bind up the brokenhearted, to proclaim liberty to the captives, and the opening of the prison to those who are bound;* (ESV)

Proverb 20:22 *Don't ever say, 'I'll get you for that!' Wait for GOD; He'll settle the score.* (The Message)

Demetri Paul Tsika, our first grandson, was born in 1992 in the great state of Texas. It was such a joy and blessing to have this little man come into this world. He has a wonderful sense of humor. He never meets a stranger. He has a gift to make people laugh. He is very confident in who he is and graduated as valedictorian from the eighth grade. He has a love for sports and has the fire of his dad.

blessing of prosperity

The Blessing: "I bless you _____ with feet that keep you positioned for blessing by walking in God's ways. I bless you with a desire for and a daily delight in God's Word. I speak favor and fruitfulness for your life as you saturate your mind with God's commandments. May you be like a tree planted by the channels of waters, so that you bear fruit and prosper, even in times when your external circumstances have created drought-like conditions. May the Lord bless you with a heart that is desirous of honoring Him with everything you have, so that He will rebuke the devourer for your sakes."

I bless you with lips that speak from a kingdom of heaven perspective. I declare, according to God's Word, that there is always abundance and not shortage; that the curse is being reversed; that you are a victor in Christ and not a victim of any circumstance; I declare that you are under kingdom order and prosperity and not under demonic disorder and poverty. You are a blessed and highly favored son/daughter. You are not cursed or a lowly despised slave."

3 John 2-4 *Beloved, I pray that all may go well with you and that you may be in good health, as it goes well with your soul. For I rejoiced greatly when the brothers came and testified to your truth, as indeed you are walking in the truth. I have no greater joy than to hear that my children are walking in the truth.* (ESV)

2 Peter 1:3, 4 *His divine power has granted to us all things that pertain to life and godliness, through the knowledge of Him who called us to His own glory and excellence, by which He has granted to us his precious and very great promises, so that through them you may become partakers of the divine nature, having escaped from the corruption that is in the world because of sinful desire.* (ESV)

Marissa Alexandra Rush was also born in the great state of Texas. God allowed Paul and me to be with Gretchen when she delivered this unique granddaughter. It's hard to believe she is now a teenager. She has a style all her own. She has a wonderful personality and is very confident, like her cousin, Demetri. She has a love for family, and she and her sisters are best friends. She is a walking fashion show and has a heart just as colorful.

blessing of victory

The Blessing: "I bless you _____ with a discerning heart that knows that the Lord is your shield. I bless you with a confidence in Christ that daily empowers you to stop listening to yourself and start speaking to yourself in the language of the kingdom of heaven: psalms, hymns & spiritual songs. I bless you with abundant life in knowing by faith and by God's grace that you may proclaim that you have the sources, forces and resources of the kingdom of heaven available to you. You can expect through your life and labors to see the kingdom come more fully. As a son/daughter in the kingdom, I bless you with a tongue that talks in terms of the authority and power available to you instead of in terms of the number and nature of those who are against you.

I bless you with a growing faith that cries to the Lord and is confident that He hears you. May you be blessed with the security that comes from trusting Father God as the One who sustains you and blesses you, because you belong to Him. May you always remember that salvation belongs to the Lord. He is the One who chose you, and He is the One who will keep you."

Psalm 84:11 *For the LORD God is a sun and shield; the LORD bestows favor and honor. No good thing does He withhold from those who walk uprightly.* (ESV)

Psalm 91:4 *His huge outstretched arms protect you— under them you're perfectly safe; His arms fend off all harm.* (ESV)

1 John 5:4 *For everyone who has been born of God overcomes the world. And this is the victory that has overcome the world-our faith.* (ESV)

On the 2nd of February 1995, Marlee Kaye Tsika joined our wonderful family. Another Texan was added to Paul and Melanie's family and another granddaughter for Paul and me. I was blessed to see her the day she was born. She was another blond, blue eyed girl. Marlee, like her sister, Emily, loves sports. She is a willing helper when it comes to serving people. She has a way of winning people over with her beautiful smile and glowing personality. She has a zest for life.

blessing of guidance

The Blessing: "May the Lord bless you _____ with a hunger for His Word so that it is always a lamp unto your feet and a light for your path. May you always use God's Word as your guide. May the Lord's good hand rest upon you so that you are confident that He will guide you continually and satisfy your desire in scorched places. May He make your bones strong so that you will be like a watered garden, like a spring of water, whose waters do not fail. I pray that in every decision you make, you will look to the only One who can and will give perfect direction for your life. May you take time to pray and get your 'marching orders' for this life. May the Word of God, not the Majority Opinion Report of Men, be the source of your thinking, speaking, and acting! May the Lord guide you with His counsel, and when your earthly journey comes to the end, may He receive the glory."

Psalm 31:3 *You're my cave to hide in, my cliff to climb. Be my safe leader, be my true mountain guide.* (The Message)

Psalm 37:23 *The steps of a good man are ordered by the Lord; and he delights in His way.* (KJV)

Isaiah 30:21 *And your ears shall hear a word behind you, saying, "This is the way, walk in it," when you turn to the right or when you turn to the left.* (ESV)

Psalm 119:105 *Your word is a lamp to guide me and a light for my path.* (GNB)

Shelby Nicole Tsika is our only Okie. She was born April 1996 in Oklahoma City. Thom and Kelley waited five years for this spunky girl. She is definitely her father made over when it comes to personality and wit. She is rather shy when it comes to meeting people (like her mom), but she is gaining courage and strength as she gets older. She has her mother's looks, but if you shut your eyes, you can hear her dad.

blessing of security

The Blessing: "My blessing for you _____ is that you do not worry about anything but pray about everything. May you daily fix your attitude with gratitude and make a choice to rejoice in all circumstances. I bless you with the confidence that when you are tempted to feel hopeless or you are in bondage to fear, you know that God is for you and has promised never to leave you or forsake you. When circumstances seem to all be bad, may you lift up praises to the only One who can change your circumstances.....the Lord our God. May you realize that God is with you in every situation and will give you strength and courage."

Philippians 4:6 *Don't fret or worry. Instead of worrying, pray. Let petitions and praises shape your worries into prayers, letting God know your concerns.* (The Message)

Deuteronomy 31:8 *God is striding ahead of you. He's right there with you. He won't let you down; He won't leave you. Don't be intimidated. Don't worry.* (The Message)

Joshua 1:9 *Haven't I commanded you? Strength! Courage! Don't be timid; don't get discouraged. God, your God, is with you every step you take.* (The Message)

Matthew 11:28-29 *Are you tired? Worn out? Burned out on religion? Come to me. Get away with me and you'll recover your life. I'll show you how to take a real rest. Walk with me and work with me—watch how I do it. Learn the unforced rhythms of grace. I won't lay anything heavy or ill-fitting on you.* (The Message)

chapter 4
A Model to Follow

The duty and privilege of blessing in the Old Testament was reserved primarily for the priest from the tribe of Levi. However, in the New Testament the priestly job is not limited to a few. Because of the work of our Lord Jesus on the cross, all true believers in Him now comprise the priesthood. As believer priests, we have been enlisted into God's Operation Blessing! We have the duty and special privilege to put God's name on others by speaking blessings. In light of the fact that the world system's curses are explicit and constant, we must not let our blessings be rare, random or vague. We are to bless our children daily in the name of the Father, Son and Holy Spirit. We are to bless one another in God's name with our declarations of friendship and love.

> *May the strength of God pilot us; may the wisdom of God instruct us; may the hand of God protect us; may the word of God direct us. Be always ours this day and evermore.*
> *Irish Quote*

Yes, curses tear down, but blessings build up. Curses weaken and shame us, but blessings give courage. Curses immobilize, but blessings energize. Our priestly calling is to bless and in so doing to put God's name on those we bless.

In the Old Testament, we find this magnificent blessing, which almost any person who has ever attended a church has heard: *"The LORD bless you and keep you; The LORD make His face to shine upon you and be gracious to you; The LORD lift up His countenance upon you and give you peace."* (Numbers 6:24-26)

No doubt, this is probably the oldest continuously used blessing in the world. It is beautiful in English, and those who know the language say that it is even more beautiful in Hebrew. In either language, there is a progression that tells us something about peace.

The structure of the blessing is remarkable. It is rhythm! It consists of three distinct parts. The blessing mounts by gradual stages to that peace which forms the most lasting and greatest gift that God can give His people. These words follow a poetic pattern. The first clause of each verse invokes God's movement toward His people. The second asks Him to act on behalf of His people. The emphasis is on the singular subject in the blessing, indicating that God's blessings come first to the community and secondly to individuals in that community.

When God gave this blessing to Moses, He instructed that Aaron — Moses' brother and the High Priest — and his sons say these words over the people of Israel. In this way God said, *"...they will put my name on the Israelites, and I will bless them."* Numbers 6:27.

Although this blessing was given to ancient Israel, it still is applicable to us today and still carries tremendous transforming ability as we hear it, receive it, repeat it and are transformed by it to experience greater depths of

God's person and provisions. In addition, we bring blessings to others as we speak God's blessings over them.

We will use it as the "Model Blessing" of the Old Testament, and demonstrate how, under grace, it will serve as scaffolding for becoming blessed, and a "blesser" of others. Here is a simple breakdown of this great model from Numbers 6:24:

The Promise of God's Favor and Protection: *The Lord bless you...*

The word for "keep" here is often used to describe guard duty, as a soldier stationed to protect his post. This is the promise of God's watchful care over us, His people, to ensure nothing happens to us apart from His loving concern.

Author Matthew Henry said, "To be under the almighty protection of God our Savior; to enjoy His favor as the smile of a loving Father, or as the cheering beams of the sun; while He mercifully forgives our sins, supplies our wants, consoles the heart, and prepares us by His grace for eternal glory; these things form the substance of this blessing, and the sum total of all blessings. In so rich a list of mercies, worldly joys are not worthy to be mentioned."

We can use this model to bless our children, our mates and our fellow Christians, as we speak this blessing over them:

The Blessing: "Father God, bless! Let your favor rest upon this child, and let him or her be enveloped by your loving care. Bless them with a confirmation of your love for them and reveal your constant watch care over them. Bless them with the eyes of faith that lets them see early and clearly, lovingly and convincingly, their absolute need for you. Capture their heart that they may gladly acknowledge that need and surrender their life to you. Bless them with true insight that enables them to realize that you are the great blessing and not things. Bless them with saving grace in order that they may know you personally and intimately in the power of your indwelling Spirit all the days of their life. Amen."

The Promise of God's Guarding and Keeping Presence —*... and keep you;*

Think of how relevant this promise was to the children of Israel as they were heading out into the dangerous wilderness. It is just as relevant for us when we are walking though the valley of the shadow of death, living life in a fallen world, surrounded by innumerable enemies, facing demonic forces of darkness seeking to sift us like wheat, crouching at our door, waiting to devour us. Moreover, here is the Lord saying, "I will keep you."

The Blessing: "Father God, I claim your promise to protect, hold, guard, sustain, and defend your own. I bless these loved ones with a relationship with you that is so inviting that you become the sum, substance, sustainer, and satisfier of their whole life. Bless them with an understanding of your nature and purpose so that they see the world, people and circumstances, through your eyes. Bless them with such confidence in you that they know your presence continuously and trust you daily in every circumstance. Bless them with the mind of Christ so that they always remember that you are their Keeper, their Shield and Defender. Amen."

The Promise of God's Face-to-Face Vision of Pleasure – *The Lord make His face to shine upon you...*

May God look at you, or turn His face toward you. The expression means, "May you enter into a face-to-face relationship with Him, a place of presence and intimacy." This is a picture of the delight of the Lord in His people and is an indication of His pleasure in them. It is an indication of His presence and His communion and His approval of His people. A scene comes to mind from the movie *Chariots of Fire*, where Eric Liddell says, "I know I was made to be a missionary to China, but when I run, I feel God's pleasure."

The "face" of God is His personality as turned towards man, or else turned away from Him. His face hidden or turned away is despair and death (Deuteronomy 31:17, 18; Job 13:24). His face turned against man is destruction and death (Leviticus 17:10; Psalm 34:16). His face turned upon man in love and mercy is life and salvation (Psalm 27:1; 44:3).

The Blessing: "Father God, bless my loved one with such an awareness of your holy personal presence that it shines like the rays of the morning sun sending light into the secret places of their heart. Bless them with the confidence and awareness that your face is turned toward them, and it has a smile upon it. Bless them with an open and honest heart-to-heart relationship with you. Bless them with eyes that clearly see the vision of what you desire them to become. Amen."

The Promise of God's Provision of Grace — ...*and be gracious to you;*

The grace of God is the hand of God's power and the heart of God's love moving toward us in mercy and measureless blessings. God the Father blesses with all spiritual blessings: electing, adopting, justifying, pardoning grace, regenerating and calling, persevering grace and eternal life. God the Son blesses particularly with redeeming grace and has a concern in all the other blessings. The saints are blessed with them in Him, they are all in His hands, they are procured by Him, come through Him, and are the gifts of His grace. God the Spirit blesses as a spirit of regeneration and sanctification, as the spirit of faith, as a comforter, as the spirit of adoption, and as the earnest (down payment) and sealer of the saints unto the day of redemption.

Author Henry Law said, "What wonders are wrapped up in grace! Its birth is in the heavens--its fruit upon the earth. It looks on those in whom no merit dwells. It sees them lost, but still it loves, and pities, and relieves. It drew salvation's scheme. It named salvation's sons. It raised the cross, and led the Savior to it. Apart from Christ--it has no being--and no admission-door to its beloved work. But now, through Christ, its visits come on sanctifying wings. The graceless become gracious, because grace works. The gracious become glorious, because grace triumphs."

The Blessing: "Father God, bless my loved ones with your amazing grace, so that they may know from experience your kindness, your favor and your total willingness to be all that they need. Bless them with a heart-hunger to cooperate with that graciousness as you take them deeper into the riches and reaches of your grace. Bless them with a desire to know you heart to heart, so that when they see you face to face you will not a be a stranger to them. Bless them with hearing ears and obedient hearts that choose your will in every circumstance. Bless them with the grace to discipline their spiritual life, take control of their thought life, and always quickly face and repent of sin. Bless them so that they recognize your favor, kindness and faithfulness to them as they learn to walk in the light. Amen."

The Promise of God's Special and Tender Interest in His People:
The Lord turn His face toward you...

The above expression means to show His face and favor. It means He looks cheerfully on His people, declares Himself well pleased with them in Christ, and appears as smiling upon them through Him, indulging them with visits of love, restoring to them the joys of His salvation, and upholding them with His free Spirit. Such awareness of God's face smiling upon us should cause us to walk pleasantly and comfortably in the ways of God, expecting eternal life and happiness, as God's free gift through Christ.

God's face is the personal manifestation of His loving presence. One's face speaks a language all its own, and when God says His face is toward His people, it means He has given them peace — peace, prosperity, completeness, health, safety, general well-being, and multitudes of other blessings as well.

This clause seems to repeat the last in a somewhat stronger form, as implying more personal and individual attention from the Lord. His face shines upon all that love Him, as the sun shines where no clouds intervene; but His face is lifted up to that soul for which He has a more special regard. To lift up the eyes or the face upon any one is to look upon that one with peculiar, special, and tender interest.

The Blessing: " Father God, bless my loved ones so that they grow in intimacy in their relationship with you as you turn your face toward them. Bless them so that this increasing intimacy draws them to higher levels of integrity and morality and is constantly purifying their values. Bless them with a depth of communion so deep and precious with you that they are ruined for anything else. Bless them so that your abundant life and Spirit-power flows more abundantly through their thoughts, words and deeds. Bless them with a desire to keep their face always turned toward your face. Amen."

The Promise of God's Provision of Peace: *...and give you peace.*

The Hebrew for peace is SHALOM. In it is all outward, needful prosperity, internal peace of mind, through the blood and righteousness of

Christ, the peacemaker, and peace giver, and eternal peace in the world to come.

The word SHALOM is both a greeting and a goodbye. The meaning of this Hebrew word for peace includes rest and restoration, safety and wholeness. The root meaning of SHALOM is restoration by the payment of a price. The Lord Jesus Christ redeemed us at the cost of His own perfect and sinless life when He died on the cross as a sacrifice to take away our sin - the price of our ransom.

Someone used the term "shalom" as an acronym:

SHALOM
Security, wholeness, safety and peace,
Heaven's favor and blessings never cease.
Always God's mercy and kindness for you,
Love, joy and truth in His Word shining through.
Only in the Lord His people find rest,
Manifold blessings of peace manifest.

Peace is not the absence of conflict but the presence of assurance that all is in God's hands, and we can rest at ease that He loves us. The peace of God only comes when we know that, despite our sinfulness, even though we offend God daily, we are still the objects of His electing love -- His favorites. It is so easy to forget the reason for this peace. The reason that God will bless and keep us and shine His grace on us, and that with a smiling face, is because He has fixed our legal problems with His holy law. The Apostle Paul sums this up in Romans 5:1, *"Since we have been justified by faith, we have peace with God through our Lord Jesus Christ."*

The Blessing: "Father God, bless my loved ones so that they live before Your face in such a manner as to know that Your face turned toward them is indicative of the peace they have with You. Bless them with the assurance that the fact that they have peace with You through our Lord Jesus Christ means that they are the center of Your love and purpose. Bless them with the stability that Your peace brings; so that they can face any challenge without wavering, through You, the Lifegiver. Bless them with a life that is anchored in peace with God, so the peace of God guards their hearts and minds from any set of circumstances. Bless them with great thoughts of a God who is large and in charge and with the certainty of safety in Your love. Amen."

The Time to Start is NOW!

It is one thing to know you can start receiving blessings today, but another thing altogether to begin receiving them. An old Chinese proverb states, "The journey of a thousand miles begins with the first step." Why not take that first step today? Begin by making sure that you are up to date in your walk with the Lord. If there is any unforgiveness that you have harbored against someone in the past, repent and release forgiveness toward them. Then ask God to bless and show favor to any person that has been your enemy or that has reviled and persecuted you. In so doing, you open the channel for God's blessings to flow.

Ask Father God to open the storehouse doors of His blessings so that you live blessed in order to be a blessing. Begin to live by faith in the daily expectation that your Heavenly Father will bless you, keep you, and cause His face to shine upon you and give you peace and every provision needed to glorify God by enjoying Him—beginning right now! Expect to be constantly moving from unforgiveness into forgiveness, from hurt into healing, from fear into faith, from peace with God to the peace of God, and from curses into blessings!

chapter 5
Making Operation Blessing a Lifestyle

The following are more personal examples that I have spoken over my loved ones. Having enlisted in God's Operation Blessing, let's go on to greater levels of learning to be like Father God, the Blessed One and the True Blesser of all men. BE BLESSED!

Bryan Ezekiel Tsika (Zeke) came along five days after his cousin, Shelby. I believe he had a smile on his face from the day he was born. He has had a spirit of laughter come on him, so that everyone around would be filled with joy and laughter. He blesses everyone he's around. He has a servant spirit. He has a grateful and thankful heart.

blessing of creativity

The Blessing: "I bless you _____ with the awareness that although God gifts every one of us differently, may you know from experience that He has blessed you with very special abilities. May you be faithful to use these 'giftings' to glorify God and encourage people. In Christ you have been enriched in every way. He does not withhold any good thing from you when you are walking in His ways. He's the One who gives favor and honor. May you acknowledge that every good and perfect gift is from Him and not something you accomplished all by yourself. I bless you with a heart that is intent upon glorifying Christ in all you do."

Psalm 84:11 *For the LORD God is a sun and shield; the LORD bestows favor and honor. No good thing does He withhold from those who walk uprightly.* (ESV)

I Peter 4:10-11 *Be generous with the different things God gave you, passing them around so all get in on it: if words, let it be God's words; if help, let it be God's hearty help. That way, God's bright presence will be evident in everything through Jesus, and He'll get all the credit as the One mighty in everything—encores to the end of time. Oh, yes!* (The Message)

Romans 12:6-8. *Let's just go ahead and be what we were made to be, without enviously or proudly comparing ourselves with each other, or trying to be something we aren't. If you preach, just preach God's Message, nothing else; if you help, just help, don't take over; if you teach, stick to your teaching; if you give encouraging guidance, be careful that you don't get bossy; if you're put in charge, don't manipulate; if you're called to give aid to people in distress, keep your eyes open and be quick to respond; if you work with the disadvantaged, don't let yourself get irritated with them or depressed by them. Keep a smile on your face.* (The Message)

Malory Amelia Rush was born to Mark and Gretchen in November 1996... their third daughter and our sixth granddaughter. She has a gift of communication!! She loves sports and singing in her church choir. You could say that she's a 'drama queen' when it comes to most things. We call her our 'love bug,' because she is a very affectionate young lady.

blessing of beauty

The Blessing: "I bless you _____ with the inner strength and dignity that comes from the Lord. May His indwelling presence so fill and flood your heart that the light of it shines through your life as you feed on His Word and hope in Him. Beauty is very fleeting! It's here today and gone tomorrow. Since we really don't know what tomorrow holds, I pray that you will trust in the Lord and let His righteousness be your beauty. Yes, take care of yourself physically but know that your inner beauty shines far greater than your outer beauty and will never grow old and ugly."

Proverbs 31:25-26, 30 *Strength and dignity are her clothing, and she smiles at the future. Charm is deceitful and beauty is vain, But a woman who fears the LORD, she shall be praised.* (ESV)

1 Peter 3:3-5 *What matters is not your outer appearance—the styling of your hair, the jewelry you wear, the cut of your clothes but your inner disposition. Cultivate inner beauty, the gentle, gracious kind that God delights in. The holy women of old were beautiful before God that way, and were good, loyal wives to their husbands. Sarah, for instance, taking care of Abraham, would address him as "my dear husband." You'll be true daughters of Sarah if you do the same, unanxious and unintimidated.* (ESV)

Thomas Jakob Tsika is our third grandson. He, like his cousin Emily, is a North Carolinian. Thom and Kelley were living in Burnsville when Jake entered this world. He is such a precious young man who is also a love bug. He loves to help around the Ranch and greet the guests when they arrive. His favorite thing is spending time with Demetri and Zeke, his heroes, and he loves to be around family.

blessing of encouragement

The Blessing: "May the Lord bless you _____ with the awareness of His presence so that you can daily encourage yourself in the Lord your God. May He make you a blessing in the lives of others as you encourage them by your kind words and deeds. As God brings someone to your heart during the day, I pray that you will be brave enough and caring enough to call and encourage them or lift them up to the Lord in prayer. I know that kind and encouraging words spoken can lift up a person who is discouraged, hopeless and feeling like no one cares. May you be blessed with the knowledge that there is no greater encouragement than to be assured of the esteem in which God holds you. May you be constantly amazed that in spite of all that we were in sin and were not in righteousness before coming to Christ; in spite of our being unworthy of the least of His mercies, He has chosen to love us and encourages us to experience, enjoy and express that life and love which the Holy Spirit imparts both now and forever."

Proverbs 12:25 *Worry weighs us down; a cheerful word picks us up.* (The Message)

2 Thessalonians 2:16-17 *May Jesus Himself and God our Father, who reached out in love and surprised you with gifts of unending help and confidence, put a fresh heart in you, invigorate your work, enliven your speech.* (ESV)

Philippians 4:6-8 *Be careful for nothing, but in everything by prayer and supplication with thanksgiving let your requests be made known unto God. And the peace of God, which passes all understanding shall keep your hearts and minds through Christ Jesus. Finally, brethren, whatsoever things are true, whatsoever things are honest, whatsoever things are just, whatsoever things are lovely, whatsoever things are pure, whatsoever things are of good report; if there be any virtue, if there be any praise, think on these things.* (ESV)

All families should have a 'surprise' package like we had arrive in 2005. Kadie Jewel Tsika, Thom and Kelley's third, is more than a surprise package. She's a joy and blessing to everyone here at the Ranch. Paul and I are getting the privilege of seeing her grow from a baby. God has blessed us with this. She comes to see us every morning, and she always has a smile on her face. She is 'Miss Bubbly.' She is always dancing and singing and bringing joy to every day.

blessing of
eternal life

The Blessing: "I bless you _____ with a heart of revelation from our Lord Jesus Christ. I bless you with the daily realization that Jesus is the Way, the Truth and the Life. May you be blessed with an understanding heart that clearly understands that eternal life is not a principle or a place but a person – Jesus. May you be blessed with the understanding that eternal life begins at salvation and continues through all eternity..

Nothing will be greater in this life than wasting or spending yourself on Jesus. He is worthy! May you be blessed with clarity of purpose regarding why Jesus did what He did -- Jesus gave His life for us, to give His life to us, to live His life through us. May you feed on Him who is the Bread of Life. May you say as Mary did when she first saw the resurrected Christ, "My Lord and My God." May your hope be in Christ alone......plus nothing, minus nothing!

I bless you with the personal awareness that if you want life, you can't leave Jesus out. If you want rest, you can't exclude Him. If you want power, you can't ignore Him. If you want light, you can't reject Him. If you seek truth, you can't reject Him. If you crave love, you can't despise Him. If you pursue joy, you can't omit Him. If you want peace, you can't resist Him. Christ is all and in all. May you daily experience Christ, not just a reference point in the margin of your life, but the very reason and resource, the sum and substance, the center and circumference of your life!"

John 6:51 *I am the Bread—living Bread!—who came down out of heaven. Anyone who eats this Bread will live—and forever! The Bread that I present to the world so that it can eat and live is myself, this flesh-and-blood self.* (The Message)

John 11:25-27 *You don't have to wait for the End. I Am, right now, Resurrection and Life. The one who believes in me, even though he or she dies, will live. And everyone who lives believing in me does not ultimately die at all. Do you believe this? Yes, Master. All along I have believed that you are the Messiah, the Son of God who comes into the world.* (The Message)

I John 5:11-12 *This is the testimony in essence: God gave us eternal life; the life is in His Son. So, whoever has the Son, has life; whoever rejects the Son, rejects life.* (The Message.

Psalm 62:1-2, 5 -7 *My soul, wait in silence for God only, for my hope is from Him. He only is my rock and my salvation, my stronghold; I shall not be shaken. On God my salvation and my glory rest; the rock of my strength, my refuge is in God.* (The Message)

I would be remiss if I didn't include our own precious children in these blessings. On earth, they have been the oxygen in our air, the fragrance in our flower, and the melody in our music. Along with their God-sent spouses, they make life for us, the grand blessing that it is.

On February 8, 1967, Paul and I became parents for the first time. Oh, what a journey we were in for with this daughter God had blessed us with…Gretchen Ann. For a few months, I didn't think she was a blessing. After all, I was 19 years old. I had no experience in caring for babies. She cried and threw up everything I fed her. I cried every time she cried! I was in pain from her delivery. I was 2,000 miles away from my mother. However, as the months rolled by, I fell in love with this little daughter. I felt like I was the most blessed of women. Here was this precious gift given to Paul and me to raise and care for, even at our young age. She was a leader from the time she was born. She has a vivacious personality and finds it easy to meet people and make them feel important. She's always had a great love for her family. As she left for Liberty University, we saw her maturity as she chose a godly man with whom to live her life. Only eternity will record how much we love Mark Alan Rush. We know God had him picked out for Gretchen from birth. We have watched him these 21 years as he's cared for, loved, provided for and led our daughter. He has had to use a big stick at times….just kidding. We see them raising three daughters in a Christian home with great values. We feel so blessed to have Gretchen Ann Rush as not just our daughter, but as a friend. She can't be replaced. This is 'ditto' for Mark.

blessing of finances

The Blessing: "May you be blessed _____ with the certainty that when the Lord is your Shepherd, you shall have no want! May you be blessed with the confidence that He will provide everything you need. Turn your heart toward Him and not toward selfish gain. Be content with the provisions of your God. He's the One who gives the power to get wealth. Don't fall into the trap of 'loving' money, but use money as a means to bless others. Since God knows even when a lowly sparrow falls from the sky, since He clothes the fields with beautiful flowers, how much more will He watch over you and know your every need! We're so much more important to Him than birds or plants. Honor the One who gives you everything you need in this life and the life to come."

Malachi 3:8-10-11 *Begin by being honest. Do honest people rob God? But you rob me day after day. You ask, 'How have we robbed you?' The tithe and the offering—that's how! And now you're under a curse—the whole lot of you—because you're robbing me. Bring your full tithe to the Temple treasury so there will be ample provisions in my Temple. Test me in this and see if I don't open up heaven itself to you and pour out blessings beyond your wildest dreams. For my part, I will defend you against marauders; protect your wheat fields and vegetable gardens against plunderers. The Message of God-of-the-Angel-Armies.* (The Message)

Philippians 4:12 *I'm just as happy with little as with much, with much as with little. I've found the recipe for being happy whether full or hungry, hands full or hands empty.* (The Message)

Psalm 119:36 *A devout life does bring wealth, but it's the rich simplicity of being yourself before God. Since we entered the world penniless and will leave it penniless, if we have bread on the table and shoes on our feet, that's enough. But if it's only money these leaders are after, they'll self-destruct in no time. Lust for money brings trouble and nothing but trouble. Going down that path, some lose their footing in the faith completely and live to regret it bitterly ever after.* (The Message)

Paul Edward Tsika II, came into this world on August 16, 1969. What a joy it was to now have a son. He was 'cotton' headed and full of fire. Paul and I were so excited; after all we were experts by now. However, this was a totally different creature than the little girl we had been enjoying for two and a half years. He loved bugs, trucks, cars and smashing things. I remember when he woke his dad up one morning with the rolling pin when he was a year old! But, after all, he's our son. It was forgiven. He had a fury in him from childhood. He struggled all through school, not only with learning, but with his temper. When he wanted to get married at 18 years

of age, we knew he was capable of taking care of a wife and children. He has always been our confident one! You name it, he can do it! We were blessed as we watched him marry a young woman of God. We encouraged him as he struggled through nine years of Bible school, Bible College, and seminary. We were proud parents when we attended his graduation from Southwestern Seminary with his Master's Degree while raising four children and sometimes working three jobs. We are very blessed to have him and his family working with us here at Restoration Ranch. Paul Edward is in charge of operations (C.O.O.) here and does all of our building. He can't be replaced. Melanie Elaine Hadden was born in Baton Rouge, Louisiana, just in time to grow up and be available for Paul Edward. She was 17 years old and had just graduated from high school when she and Paul married. She has walked with him through all of the years of his schooling, serving in churches as youth pastor and as a pastor. She has joyfully followed him wherever he felt God leading them as a family. We praise God for this godly young woman who has faithfully loved and served the Lord. She can't be replaced.

blessing of forgiveness

The Blessing: "I bless you _____ with the assurance that you have been graced by our God who blots out your transgressions, for His own sake, and remembers your sins no more (Isaiah 43:25). Since Christ has cleansed you and made you whole, may you bless others by being compassionate to them and forgiving them the same way God in Christ forgave you.

I bless you with the daily discernment that unforgiveness is death on the installment plan! May you clearly know that love cannot last long or live out its eternal purpose in relationships without a foundation of forgiveness.

Forgiveness is a promise made. It is a choice of the will. Having a forgiving spirit means that you are willing to absorb the cost and loss of the offenses against you. Forgiveness is a full pardon and an act of love based upon God's having forgiven you.

May you be blessed by seeing clearly that you cannot live with purpose and joy unless you love; you will not be able to love unless you forgive; and you will not forgive unless your hatred is melted by the searing truth and grace of the gospel!"

I John 1:9 *On the other hand, if we admit our sins—make a clean breast of them—He won't let us down; He'll be true to Himself. He'll forgive our sins and purge us of all wrongdoing.* (The Message)

Isaiah 55:6, 7 *Seek the LORD while He may be found; call upon Him while He is near; let the wicked forsake his way, and the unrighteous man his thoughts; let him return to the LORD, that He may have compassion on him, and to our God, for He will abundantly pardon.* (ESV)

Mark 11:25 *And when you assume the posture of prayer, remember that it's not all asking. If you have anything against someone, forgive—only then will your heavenly Father be inclined to also wipe your slate clean of sins.* (The Message)

When Thomas James Tsika came along February 25, 1972, we were oh so thrilled. This little tender hearted boy was such a joy to have in our home. He has always been our little comedian. He kept us laughing with all his antics. Of course, he came with a gift of agitation, also. When we moved from Louisiana where he spent most of his younger years, we never heard a complaint from him. He was leaving all he knew, yet he moved willingly. We were blessed when he went to work as a bag boy at Harris Teeter Grocery Store in Asheville, North Carolina. He also worked at the Grove Park Inn and Country Club as a bellman. He was willing to do anything he could to help us. We were amazed as we watched him take up golf and accomplish so much in that field. We were proud parents as we watched him get his degree from Mars Hill College in North Carolina, work as an assistant golf pro at Mountain Air Country Club, and then become the golf coach at Mars Hill College. We are blessed to have Thom as our CFO, and to have his family here at Restoration Ranch. He can't be replaced. We were thrilled when he and Kelley Lynne Stamey decided to get married in 1991. I spotted Kelley at church not long after we moved to Asheville. I pointed her out to Paul, and he agreed with me that this was the girl Thom needed to meet. She is a quiet young woman...quite different than the Tsika Family. However she chose to be a part of this clan. She is a home body, yet she has learned to be comfortable around 'lots' of people as she serves here at the Ranch with us. She is a loving, caring wife and mother of three beautiful children. She can't be replaced.

blessing of friendship

The Blessing: "I bless you _____ with the comfort of knowing that you are a blessed person if you have many friends, for a true friend loves no matter what you are going through and no matter how you act. May you be blessed with friends that multiply your joys, divide your grief, and whose honesty is always firm. May you know that prosperity begets friends, but adversity proves them. May you have a friend who comes in when the whole world has gone out. Friends are people with whom you dare to be yourself. Your soul can be naked with them. They ask you to put on nothing, only to be what you are. When you are with them, you feel as a prisoner feels that has been declared innocent. You do not have to be on your guard.

friendship (frend·ship) the state of being friends 2. a mutual union or bond felt between people who care deeply for one another

My prayer is that God will give you a true friend who will be honest with you even when it is 'hurtful' and brings pain. I pray that you will have a friend who will give you wise (God's) counsel in every situation. You are God's, so I pray that you will be a true friend to many as you travel this life."

Proverbs 17:17 *Friends love through all kinds of weather, and families stick together in all kinds of trouble.* (The Message)

Proverbs 27:6 *Faithful are the wounds of a friend, Wounds from a friend can be trusted...* (The Message)

John 15:13 *Greater love has no one than this, that one lay down his life for his friends.* (The Message)

Proverbs 25:21, 22 *If you see your enemy hungry, go buy him lunch; if he's thirsty, bring him a drink. Your generosity will surprise him with goodness, and GOD will look after you.* (The Message)

My husband, Paul, is my greatest blessing on this earth. God knew exactly who I needed in my life to make me who I am today. He is not only my encourager, but he has been an encourager to so many. He has a way of lifting up anyone who is discouraged. He gives hope to people, because he knows how to edify with words. He is one of the biggest givers I've ever known. He knows how to believe God in every circumstance in which we find ourselves. He has always gone out of his way to visit friends who need a 'word' of encouragement. He loves me, his children and his grandchildren with a love that's beyond words. He is the wisest man I know. I know this to be true, because he gets his 'wisdom' from God's Word. He has a genuine love for Jesus and a heart to serve our Lord and His people. Am I say-

ing that he has never disappointed me? Absolutely not! What I am saying is that he has a heart to repent when he is wrong, and he also has a heart to get past the failure and keep on keeping on. He has never been one to wallow in pity or self abasement. He simply asks for forgiveness and gets back into the fight. I am a blessed woman to be loved by such a man.

blessing of love

The Blessing: "I bless you _____ with a heart that will love the Lord your God with all of your being and your neighbor as yourself. Jesus said that this is the greatest commandment. May you be blessed to know from daily experience God's love which is that spirit of life that gives without regard to cost to meet the actual needs of another, asking nothing in return!

May you realize that the greatest honor you can give Father God is to live joyfully because of the knowledge of His love.

Define yourself as one beloved of God, knowing that it is His love for you, and His choice of you, that make up your worth. Stand anchored in God, before whom you stand naked, with nothing to offer Him but your own wicked, deceitful heart – and hear this God, your Heavenly Father say to you -- 'You are my son/daughter, my beloved one. You are worth Jesus to me because that is how much I paid for you!'

May His love so permeate your heart that it will be the overflow of your life. I pray that you will express your love to the Lord by speaking well of Him and praising Him....thanking Him, worshipping Him, enjoying Him, letting Him know that He is altogether lovely. I pray that you will love the unlovely....just as God did with us when He sent His son to die for us even when we were sinners."

John 3:16 *For God so loved the world, that He gave His only begotten Son, that whoever believes in Him shall not perish, but have eternal life.* (KJV)

John 15:9 *I've loved you the way my Father has loved me. Make yourselves at home in my love.* (The Message)

I John 4:19 *We love, because He first loved us.* (ESV)

Luke 6:32-35 *If you only love the lovable, do you expect a pat on the back? Run-of-the-mill sinners do that. If you only help those who help you, do you expect a medal? Garden-variety sinners do that. If you only give for what you hope to get out of it, do you think that's charity? The stingiest of pawnbrokers does that. I tell you, love your enemies. Help and give without expecting a return. You'll never--I promise--regret it. Live out this God-created identity the way our Father lives toward us, generously and graciously, even when we're at our worst.* (The Message)

For those of you who have read this little book, I pray that it will not be the end, but the beginning of a life that "blesses and curses not!"

In conclusion, I am asking our Heavenly Father to make real the blessing that I am now going to speak over you since it is obvious that you are desirous of learning to bless others because you took the time to read this book.

The Blessing: "Father, I speak blessings over all those who have taken time to read this little book. I ask that You bless them with a heart that loves You — the Ultimate Blesser -- more than Your blessings. Bless them with joy and peace in believing, so that they may abound in true hope. Bless them with health and prosperity even as their hearts delight in You. Bless them by opening the eyes of their hearts in order to see that they are never more like You than when they are blessing others with the sincere words of their lips and the practical good works of their hands. Bless them by filling them with Your Spirit, so that they have the discipline to become daily blessers of others, especially those of the household of faith and their own families. Bless them with the peace and assurance that the best is always ahead for the child of God, and when they draw their last breath in this life, they will be forever with You in the land of perfect day! Amen."

Now, watch as God ministers, encourages, lifts up, edifies, heals and changes those you bless. He will give them a greater desire to do right and live right and be everything you speak over them. *"And God said ...and it was so."* (Genesis 1)

You are blessed and very much so. Now, go forth and multiply and replenish by being a blesser and a blessing.

family gallery

Paul in Little League as a boy.

Billie Kaye in 3rd grade.

Billie, 1965 (I think the glasses are back in style.)

Paul, 1962 graduation

March 1966, right after Paul proposed.
Paul was a driver for Recruit Classification.
I was a secretary with Recruit Training.

Our first home.

Gretchen, Thom and Paul Edward, 1976

Family photo, about 1976.

Family... every year the kids grow up, and we grow older (and more mature, hah!); 1979

We're still smiling! Paul Edward, Gretchen, Thom, Paul & Billie. 1983.

Mark, Gretchen and girls

Paul, Melanie and their family

Marissa, Malory, Gretchen & Meagan (left to right)

Jake, Kelley, Kadie, Thom & Shelby (left to right)

A pile of grandkids!

Jake and dad.

Future praise leader, Zeke

Happy kids, Malory, Marlee, Zeke & Marissa

Baseballer Jake

Baby Kadie, with a look of surprise!

Lined up, ready to eat together.
Demetri, Marlee, Emily & Zeke

Shelby, cool in her shades.

Jake, Shelby and Kadie

MERRY

1. LIVELY: FULL OF FUN
2. *festive or to be festive*
3. to have fun
4. cheerfulness

April birthdays!

Demetri and Emily, stylin' it.

Shelby, Marlee, Marissa and Kadie. Practicing for High School Prom

Our home, Restoration Ranch.

Demetri at the Ranch

Jet-skiing on the lake.

Paul Edward and sons

Mudding at Senderos.

Rush bunch on the Waverunner

Our grandsons

Meagan Rush

Malory, our fashion designer

Shelby and Kadie, sisters.

celebrate (sel´·e·brat) 1. perform as a ritual 2. to commemorate with festivity 3. to do honor to 4. have a good time

[cel´·ebrate]
to commemorate with festivity

FOREVER (for·ev´·er) 1. for always, without end 2. without the bonds of time; eternal

inspire (in·spir´) I. to stimulate or impel, as to some creative effort 2. to motivate as by divine influence

LOVE *1. strong liking or affection of something or someone* 2. a passionate affection from one person to another 3. the object of such affection: a sweetheart

legacy (leg´·e·se) something passed through a family, handed down as from an ancestor

reminisce (rem´·e·nis) to think, talk or write about remembered events, usually with fondness

BELIEVE (be·leve´) 1. to put one's trust in 2. to accept as fact 3. to have faith in *togetherness*

TOGETHERNESS (to·geth´·ur·nes) 1. the spending of much time together, resulting in a more unified bond